THE ULTIMATE GUIDE TO WRITING

Your First Children's Book

Including Five Bonus Sample Styles to Inspire Your Creative Journey

BY ANNIE GIBBINS

Copyright © 2023 by **Annie Gibbins**
All rights reserved. No part of this publication may be reproduced, distributed or transmitted in any form or by any means, without prior written permission.

Annie Gibbins / Women's Biz Publishing
New South Wales, Australia
www.womensbizpublishing.com

All rights reserved. No part of this book may be used or reproduced by any means, graphic, electronic, or mechanical, including photocopying, recording, taping or by any information storage retrieval system without the written permission of the copyright owner except in the case of brief quotations embodied in critical articles and reviews. Because of the dynamic nature of the Internet, any web addresses or links contained in this book may have changed since publication and may no longer be valid. The views expressed in this work are solely those of the author and do not necessarily reflect the views of the publisher and the publisher hereby disclaims any responsibility for them.

Book Layout © 2023 womensbizpublishing.com
The Ultimate Guide to Writing Your First Children's Book / Annie Gibbins -- 1st ed.
Paperback ISBN 978-1-922969-02-6

womensbizglobal.com

Welcome to the wonderful world of writing children's books!

Whether you're a seasoned writer or just starting out, writing for children can be an incredibly rewarding and exciting experience. From picture books to middle-grade novels, there is a wide range of genres and styles to explore when writing for young readers.

In this book, we'll cover everything you need to know to get started on your journey as a children's book author. We'll explore the elements of a great children's book, from characters and plot, to pacing and dialogue. We'll also dive into the business side of writing, including finding an agent and submitting your work to publishers.

But first, let's talk about why writing for children is so special. Children's books have the power to ignite a lifelong love of reading in young readers, to inspire imagination and creativity, and to teach valuable life lessons in a way that is both entertaining and memorable. As a children's book author, you have the opportunity to shape the minds and hearts of future generations. Whether you're writing a funny picture book about a talking animal, or a heartfelt, middle-grade novel about friendship and loss, your words have the power to make a difference in the lives of your readers.

So, let's begin. Whether you're writing for your own children, for a classroom of students, or for a wider audience, this book will provide you with the tools and inspiration you need to bring your stories to life. From brainstorming and outlining plots, to drafting and editing, we'll guide you through the entire writing process, step by step.

Get ready to embark on an exciting adventure into the wonderful world of writing children's books.

CONTENTS

CHAPTER 1
Introduction 1
CHAPTER 2
Idea Generation 9
CHAPTER 3
Developing Your Characters 13
CHAPTER 4
Plot and Structure 19
CHAPTER 5
Writing Style and Voice 27
CHAPTER 6
Editing and Revision 33
CHAPTER 7
Illustrations and Design 37
CHAPTER 8
Publishing and Promotion 42
CHAPTER 9
Challenge and Obstacles You May Encounter 46
CHAPTER 10
Over to You 52
BONUS MATERIAL 55

CHAPTER 1

INTRODUCTION

Welcome to the wonderful world of writing children's books. If you're considering writing a children's book, you're about to embark on a fulfilling and creative journey that can bring joy and knowledge to young readers. In this guide, we'll explore the process of writing a children's book, from idea generation, to publishing and promotion. Whether you're a first-time author or a seasoned writer, get ready to unleash your creativity and start writing a children's book that will inspire, educate, and entertain young readers.

Writing a children's book can have many benefits beyond the joy of creating something new. It can be a powerful way to connect with children and inspire them to read and learn. Children's books have the ability to introduce complex topics and ideas, in a way that is accessible and engaging for young readers, helping to expand their knowledge and worldview. Moreover, writing a children's book can also be a lucrative venture, with the potential for financial success and even a career as an author.

But before you can start writing, it's important to understand the different types of children's books and the importance of knowing your audience. Children's books come in many different forms, from picture books for very young readers, to middle-grade novels for older children. Understanding the different types of children's books, as well as the age range of your audience, is important in order to create a story that will engage and entertain.

Knowing your audience also is crucial to writing a successful children's book. It's important to understand a child's interests, what they find funny or engaging, and the level of complexity they can handle. For example, a book for young children will be more focused on visual storytelling and simple language, while one for older children may have more complex plots and themes.

In this guide, we'll cover everything you need to know to write a compelling and engaging children's book, including idea generation, character development, plot and structure, writing style and voice, editing and revising, illustrations and design, and publishing and promotion. By the end of this guide, you'll have a better understanding of the steps involved in writing a children's book and be ready to bring your ideas to life.

So, whether you're writing for personal fulfilment or professional gain, the key to success in children's book writing is a deep understanding of your audience. By knowing what young readers enjoy and what they need from a book, you can craft a story that will capture their imaginations and leave a lasting impression. So, let's dive into the wonderful world of writing children's books and discover how you can create stories that will entertain, educate, and inspire young readers.

The Benefits of Writing a Children's Book

Writing a children's book can be an incredibly rewarding experience that offers many benefits, to both the writer and the young readers who enjoy them. Here are some of the key benefits of writing a children's book:

Making a Difference

Children's books have the power to shape young minds, influence their thoughts, and spark their imagination. By writing a children's book, you have the opportunity to make a positive impact on young readers' lives and instil important values and lessons.

Developing Creativity

Writing a children's book requires creativity, imagination, and a unique perspective on life. Through the writing process, you can explore new ideas, experiment with different writing styles, and unleash your creativity in ways you may not have thought possible.

Personal Satisfaction

Seeing your book in print and knowing that it has the potential to bring joy to young readers can be incredibly satisfying. Writing a children's book is a significant accomplishment that can boost your confidence and sense of personal satisfaction.

Financial Rewards

While writing children's books may not make you a millionaire overnight, it can be a financially rewarding experience. With the right marketing and promotion, your book can become a bestseller and generate a significant income.

Building a Legacy

Children's books have the ability to leave a lasting impact on generations to come. By writing a children's book, you can leave a legacy that will be enjoyed by many young readers time and time again. Overall, writing a children's book can be a fulfilling and meaningful experience that offers many benefits. Whether you're looking to make a difference in the world, unleash your creativity, or build a successful career, writing a children's book is a great way to achieve your goals.

Different Types of Children's Books

Children's books come in many different forms, each with its own unique style, structure, and content. Here are some of the most common types of children's books:

Picture Books

Picture books are designed for very young children, typically aged three to seven to years old. They are heavily illustrated, with minimal text, and often use simple language to tell a story or convey a message.

Board Books

Board books are similar to picture books but are designed to be sturdy and durable enough for very young children to handle. They are often made of thick cardboard and have rounded corners to prevent injuries.

Early Readers

Early readers are designed for children who are just learning to read. They typically have simple sentences and easy-to-read text, with illustrations that support the text.

Chapter Books

Chapter books are longer and more complex than early readers, with multiple chapters that tell a complete story. They are typically aimed at children aged seven to 12 years old, and often deal with more complex themes and issues.

Middle-Grade Novels

Middle-grade novels are longer and more complex than chapter books, typically aimed at children aged eight to 12 years old. They often deal with more serious themes and issues and may include elements of fantasy, or science fiction.

Young Adult Novels

Young adult novels are designed for older children and teenagers, typically aged 12 to 18 years old. They deal with more mature themes and issues, and often explore complex emotional and psychological issues.

Each type of children's book has its own unique target audience, style, and structure. By understanding the different types of children's books and the age range of your audience, you can create a book that will engage and entertain young readers and leave a lasting impression.

The Importance of Knowing your Audience

Knowing your audience is critical when it comes to writing a children's book. Children have different developmental stages, interests, as well as levels of understanding, which means that a story that captivates one age group, may not necessarily appeal to another.

It is crucial to keep in mind the age range of your audience and tailor your writing to their needs. For example, a book intended for very young children may focus on simple language, repetition and visual storytelling, whereas a book aimed at older children may incorporate more complex themes, characters, and plots. Knowing what appeals to your audience is key to creating a story that engages and entertains them.

Understanding your audience also involves being aware of cultural differences, values, and beliefs. Writing a children's book that is respectful and inclusive of diverse cultures and backgrounds can help to broaden children's horizons and foster empathy and understanding.

Ultimately, writing a children's book that resonates with its intended audience has a profound impact on young readers. It can inspire a love of reading and learning, promote social and emotional growth, and even instil valuable life lessons. By taking the time to understand your audience, you can create a story that connects with them on a deeper level and leaves a lasting impression.

Inspirational Cover Design

CHAPTER TWO

IDEA GENERATION

> *To engage young readers, choose a topic that ignites your own passion. If you are passionate about your subject matter, your enthusiasm will be contagious."* - Kate Messner

Every great children's book begins with a great idea. In this chapter, we will explore different methods for finding inspiration and generating ideas for your story. We will also discuss brainstorming techniques and how to choose a topic that will engage young readers.

Finding Inspiration

Finding inspiration for your story is an important part of the creative process. Inspiration can come from a variety of sources such as personal experiences, current events, historical events, nature, or even other books.

One way to find inspiration is to think about what interests you, or what you are passionate about. Write down a list of topics or themes that you enjoy discussing or feel strongly about. This can be anything from animals, to sports, to social issues. You can also draw inspiration from your own life experiences, or the experiences of those around you.

Another way to find inspiration is to read widely and stay up to date on current events. Reading other children's books can also be a great source of inspiration, as it can help you identify trends in the market and see what types of stories are resonating with young readers.

It's important to keep an open mind when looking for inspiration and not to limit yourself to one particular source. Inspiration can come from unexpected places, so be open to new experiences and ideas.

Ultimately, the key to finding inspiration is to stay curious and observant. Pay attention to the world around you and look for stories in everyday life. With the right mindset and approach, inspiration can be found anywhere.

Once you have found your inspiration, it's time to start brainstorming ideas for your story.

Brainstorming Techniques

Brainstorming is a key step in the process of generating ideas for your children's book. Here are some techniques to help you get started:

Freewriting: This technique involves setting a timer for a specific amount of time, say 10-15 minutes, and writing down whatever comes to your mind without stopping or censoring yourself. This can help you get past any creative blocks and may also generate spontaneous and unexpected ideas.

1. Mind Mapping: Mind mapping is a visual technique that involves creating a diagram or flowchart of ideas. You start by writing down a central idea, then branch off into sub-topics and ideas related to the central theme. This can help you organise your thoughts and make connections between different ideas.
2. List Making: Making a list of potential ideas can be a quick and simple way to jumpstart your creativity. Write down any potential story ideas, character traits, settings, or themes that

come to mind. Don't worry about the quality of the ideas at first, just focus on getting them down on paper.
3. Idea Jar: This is a fun and interactive way to generate ideas. Write down story prompts or ideas on slips of paper and place them in a jar. Whenever you need inspiration, pull out a slip of paper and use that as the basis for your writing.
4. Observation: Sometimes inspiration can come from simply observing the world around you. Pay attention to children's interests and behaviours, what they find engaging and what they struggle with. This may help you generate ideas that will resonate with your chosen target audience.

Remember, the goal of brainstorming is to come up with as many ideas as possible, without self-censorship or judgement. Once you have a collection of ideas, you can evaluate them and choose the ones that best fit your vision for your children's book.

Choosing the Right Topic

Choosing a topic that will engage young readers is essential to the success of your children's book. Children are curious and have vivid imaginations, so it is important to choose a topic that captures their attention and sparks their interest. Here are some tips for choosing a topic that will engage young readers:

1. Think about the age range of your audience: The topic you choose will depend on the age range of your readers. For example, a picture book for very young readers may focus on concepts such as colours, shapes, or counting, while a chapter book for older children may explore more complex themes, like friendship, identity, or coming of age.
2. Consider your own interests and passions: Writing about something you are passionate about can help make your story

more engaging and authentic. If you love animals, consider writing a book about a group of adventurous animals on a quest. If you are interested in history, consider writing a historical fiction novel set in a particular time period.

3. Draw inspiration from real-life experiences: Your own experiences can provide a rich source of material for your story. Think about a memorable moment from your childhood, or an experience that has stayed with you over the years. You can also draw inspiration from the experiences of children you know, or even from news stories.

4. Look for gaps in the market: Take a look at the current market of children's books and try to identify gaps you can fill. Maybe there aren't enough books about a certain topic, or there is a lack of diversity in characters. By filling these gaps, you can create a unique and valuable contribution to the children's book market.

Once you have a general idea for your story, it's important to start thinking about the plot, characters, and setting. Ask yourself questions such as, "What is the problem my characters will face?" and "What is the lesson I want to teach?" This will help you to develop a strong foundation for your story.

Remember, the most important thing is to have fun and let your creativity guide you. Don't be afraid to take risks and try new things. You never know where your imagination may lead you.

In the next chapter, we'll explore how to develop relatable characters that will capture your audience's hearts and minds.

CHAPTER THREE

DEVELOPING YOUR CHARACTERS

> *"Dialogue is not just about what your characters say, it's about who they are. Use dialogue to reveal your characters' personalities, beliefs, and motivations." - J.K. Rowling*

Your characters are the driving force behind your story. They are the ones who will capture the imaginations of young readers and keep them engaged whilst reading. Therefore, creating relatable and well-developed characters is crucial to the success of your children's book.
One way to create relatable characters is to draw inspiration from your own life experiences or people you know. Think about the traits, quirks, and personalities that make them unique and incorporate those into your characters. Additionally, consider giving your characters goals, flaws and motivations that readers can identify with.

Creating Relatable Characters

Creating relatable characters is essential to engaging young readers and keeping them interested in your story. Relatable characters are those that readers can connect with on a personal level, because they share similar experiences, emotions, or personality traits.

To create such characters, it's important to consider their backstory and personality traits. What motivates them? What are their fears and desires? What are their strengths and weaknesses? Answering these questions can help you create well-rounded characters that readers can empathise with.

Another important aspect of creating relatable characters is to give them flaws. Characters that are too perfect, or those who always make the right decisions, can come across as uninteresting or unrealistic. Instead, give your characters flaws that make them relatable and human.

Finally, consider the age of your target audience when creating your characters. Younger readers may relate more to characters that are their own age or slightly older, while older readers may appreciate characters who are going through experiences similar to their own.

In summary, creating relatable characters involves developing their backstory, personality traits, and flaws, as well as considering the age of your target audience. By doing so, you can create characters that young readers will connect with and become invested in, throughout your story.

The Role of Dialogue in Character Development

Dialogue is a powerful tool in developing characters, as it allows readers to hear the character's thoughts, feelings and motivations through their words and interactions with others. Dialogue can reveal a character's personality, background and values, as well as their relationships with other characters.

To create effective dialogue, it's important to think about the character's voice and how they would realistically speak in different situations. A character's dialogue should be consistent with their personality, background and the situation they're in. For example, a shy character might speak softly and avoid eye contact, while a confident character might speak loudly and assertively.

Dialogue can also be used to advance the plot and create conflict or tension. By having characters express different opinions or goals, the story can become more complex and interesting.

It's important to remember that dialogue should always serve a purpose and move the story forward. Avoid including unnecessary dialogue or long monologues that don't add to the character or plot development. Additionally, make sure that the dialogue is age-appropriate and understandable for your target audience.

By using dialogue effectively, you can create characters that come to life on the page and engage young readers in your story.

How to Avoid Stereotypes and Create Diverse Characters

As an author in the field of children's literature, I cannot stress enough the importance of creating diverse characters in your stories. Children deserve to see themselves and others who look like them represented in literature, and it's crucial to avoid stereotyping certain groups. Instead, create characters that are multidimensional and complex.

One way to achieve this is through research and enhancing your understanding of different cultures and backgrounds. It's a good idea to also seek feedback from individuals who are part of the groups you want to represent, to ensure authenticity and accuracy.

When creating diverse characters, it's essential to consider how different aspects of their identity intersect. For example, a character who is both a person of colour and disabled, will have unique experiences that differ from someone who only identifies with one of those groups. Understanding and portraying these intersections accurately, can add depth and authenticity to your characters.

It's also crucial to avoid shallow characterisations based solely on race or ethnicity. Instead, focus on creating characters that have a unique personality, interests and experiences that make them who they are. By doing so, you can avoid perpetuating harmful stereotypes.

While race and ethnicity are crucial aspects of diversity, it's also essential to consider other factors, such as gender identity, sexuality and socioeconomic status. Including characters that represent different backgrounds and experiences will help readers understand and empathise with people from all walks of life.

Another important factor to keep in mind is cultural appropriation, which involves using elements of a culture that are not your own, without proper understanding or respect. It's vital to do your research and seek feedback to ensure that you are representing cultures in an appropriate and respectful manner.

Key areas to consider are:

Including Diverse Creators

To ensure accurate representation and avoid harmful stereotypes, it's also important to include diverse creators in the creation of children's books. This includes authors, illustrators, and editors from a variety of backgrounds and perspectives.

Addressing Microaggressions

While it's essential to avoid harmful stereotypes, it's also important to address microaggressions that can appear in children's literature. These are subtle forms of discrimination that can perpetuate harmful ideas and stereotypes. By addressing and avoiding these microaggressions, children's literature can create a more inclusive and equitable representation of diverse communities.

In conclusion, creating diverse characters not only benefits children by allowing them to see themselves and others represented in literature but also promotes empathy and understanding of different cultures and perspectives. As authors, we have a responsibility to accurately and respectfully represent the diversity that exists in our world and children's books are not an exception to this role.

Inspirational Cover Design

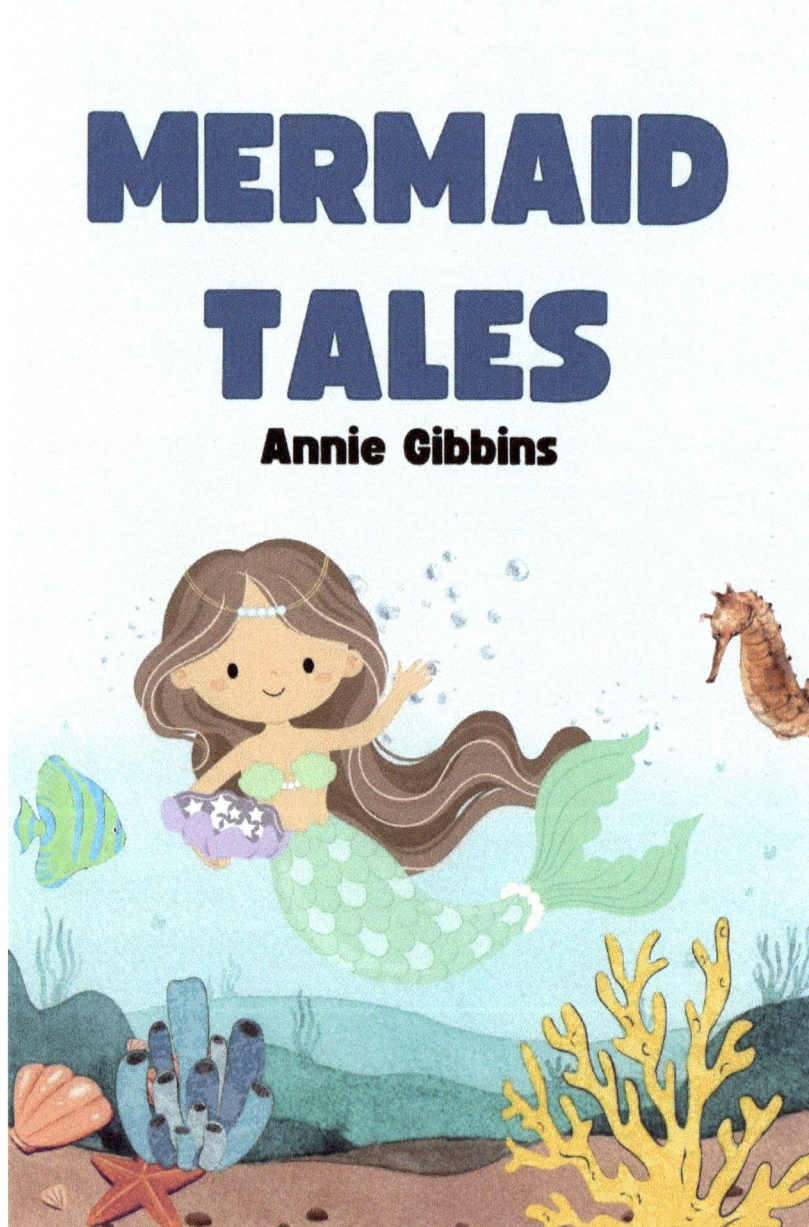

CHAPTER FOUR

PLOT AND STRUCTURE

> *"The beginning of your story should draw readers in, the middle should keep them interested, and the end should leave them satisfied. Think of it like a rollercoaster."* - Jeff Kinney

A well-structured plot is essential for keeping children engaged in a story. This takes into consideration the introduction of characters, the setting, the problem, the rising action, the climax, the falling action, and the resolution. So, let's examine all of the elements you can use to create a story that young readers will enjoy and remember.

Plot and Structure

A good plot is essential to keep children engaged and interested in a story. Whether it's a picture book or a chapter book, a well-structured plot can make all the difference. In this chapter, we will outline the elements of a children's book plot, developing a beginning, middle, and end, as well as how to choose the right point of view.

The Beginning

The beginning of a children's book should introduce the characters and the setting. It should also establish the problem that the characters will face. A strong beginning will grab the reader's attention and make them want to keep reading.

The Middle

The middle of a children's book is where the majority of the action takes place. This is where the characters work to solve the problem introduced in the beginning. The middle should include rising action, which builds tension and leads to the story's climax.

The End

The end of a children's book should resolve the problem introduced in the beginning. It should also provide a satisfying conclusion for the reader. Although the end can include a final plot twist, it should not leave any unfinished storylines.

Choosing the Right Point of View

The point of view is the perspective from which the story is told and is essential for creating a compelling story. In children's books, it's common to use either first person or third person point of view. First-person point of view is when the story is told from the perspective of one of the characters. This can help the reader connect with the character and understand their thoughts and feelings. Third-person point of view is when the story is told from an outside perspective. This can allow for a broader view of the story and can give insight into multiple characters' thoughts and feelings.

Elements of the Plot

The elements of a children's book plot typically include an introduction, rising action, climax, falling action, and resolution. These elements work together to create a coherent and engaging story for young readers.

Introduction

The introduction is the beginning of the story where the setting, characters and conflict are introduced. This is where the reader gets a sense of what the story will be about and the main characters. It's important to make this part of the plot interesting and engaging in order to grab the reader's attention.

Rising Action

The rising action is the part of the plot where conflict begins to develop, and the story starts to build momentum. This is where the reader becomes more aware of the characters and the situation they are in. The rising action should be carefully crafted to create tension and suspense, making the reader eager to continue reading to find out what happens next.

Climax

The climax is the highest point of tension in the story. This is where the conflict comes to a head and the outcome of the story is determined. It's important to make the climax exciting and surprising, to keep the reader invested in the story.

Falling Action

The falling action is the part of the plot where the conflict begins to resolve and the story winds down. This is where loose ends are tied up, and the reader gets a sense of closure. It's important to make the falling action satisfying and enjoyable as it is a crucial element to your story.

Resolution

The resolution is the end of the story, where everything is wrapped up and the conflict is resolved. This is where the reader feels a sense of what the characters have learned and how they have grown throughout the story. It's important to make the resolution satisfying and meaningful for the reader. When crafting a children's book plot, it's important to keep in mind the age and reading level of your target audience. For younger children, the plot may need to be simpler and easier to understand, while older children may be able to handle more complex storylines. Regardless of the age group, it's important to create a plot that is engaging, interesting, as well as a clear beginning, middle and end.

Developing a Beginning, Middle and End

Developing a beginning, middle and end, is an essential part of creating a cohesive and engaging plot in a children's book. The beginning sets up the story by introducing the characters, setting and conflict. It's where the reader first becomes invested in the story and is essential to hooking their attention. The middle of the story is where the bulk of the action takes place, and the conflict begins to unfold. This is where the main character faces challenges and obstacles that push the story forward. It's essential to keep the pace of the story moving in the middle section to avoid losing the reader's attention. The end of the story is where the conflict is resolved, and loose ends are tied up. This section should provide a satisfying conclusion for the reader, whether it's a happy, sad, or bittersweet ending. It should also provide a sense of closure and leave the reader with a lasting impression of both the characters and your book in general.

It's crucial to remember that each section should flow smoothly into the next, and the story should build toward a satisfying conclusion. This can be achieved through a well-crafted plot that has a clear beginning, middle, and end. One way to ensure the story flows smoothly is by creating a story outline before writing, which can help you stay on track and keep the pacing consistent.

In addition to a clear beginning, middle and end, it's important to include key plot elements that create tension and keep the reader engaged. These elements Consist of a central conflict, rising action, a climax and a resolution.

The central conflict is the problem or challenge the main character faces. The rising action builds up tension and suspense leading up to the climax, which is the point of highest tension or drama in the story. The resolution follows the climax and shows how the conflict is resolved.

Choosing the Right Point of View

Choosing the right point of view is a critical aspect of developing a compelling children's book plot. The point of view refers to the perspective from which the story is told, and the voice you choose, can greatly impact the reader's experience.

The three main types of point of view in literature are first, second and third person. In children's books, first and third person are the most commonly used points of view.

First person point of view involves telling the story through the eyes of the protagonist, using pronouns such as, "I" and "We." This point of view can create a sense of intimacy and immediacy, as the reader experiences the story through the character's thoughts and emotions. It can be an effective choice for stories that focus on character development and internal struggles. However, it can also limit the reader's perspective to only what the protagonist knows and experiences.

Second person point of view is not commonly used in children's literature but can be effective when done well. It involves addressing the reader directly and immersing them in the story, by making them the protagonist. This can create a sense of immediacy and involvement that can be particularly engaging for young readers. However, it can be challenging to maintain this perspective throughout an entire book, and it can also be challenging to create a character that the reader can fully identify with.

As such, it's important to carefully consider whether second person is the best choice for your story and target audience. If you do choose to use second person, make sure to use it consistently throughout the book and avoid switching perspectives. Additionally, ensure that the reader feels fully immersed in the story and has a clear understanding of the character they are meant to be. So, while the second person can be an effective tool in children's literature, it should be used thoughtfully and with careful consideration of the story and audience.

Third person point of view involves telling the story from an outside perspective, using pronouns such as, "He," "She," and "They." This point of view allows for a broader perspective, as the narrator can provide information and insights that the protagonist may be unfamiliar with. It can also allow for multiple perspectives, as the story can shift between different characters' experiences. However, third person point of view can create a sense of distance between the reader and the characters and may not create the same level of emotional connection as a first-person point of view.

When choosing the point of view for a children's book, it's important to consider the age and reading level of the target audience, as well as the story's content and themes. Younger children may find first person point of view more accessible and engaging, while older children may be able to handle more complex narratives told through third person point of view. It's also important to consider the tone and style of the story, as different points of view can create different moods and atmospheres.

Key Takeaway

Choosing the right point of view is an important aspect of developing a children's book plot. The point of view can impact the reader's perspective, emotional connection to the characters and the overall experience of the story. When selecting a point of view, it's important to consider the age and reading level of the target audience, the story's content, and themes, as well as the desired tone and style.

Inspirational Cover Design

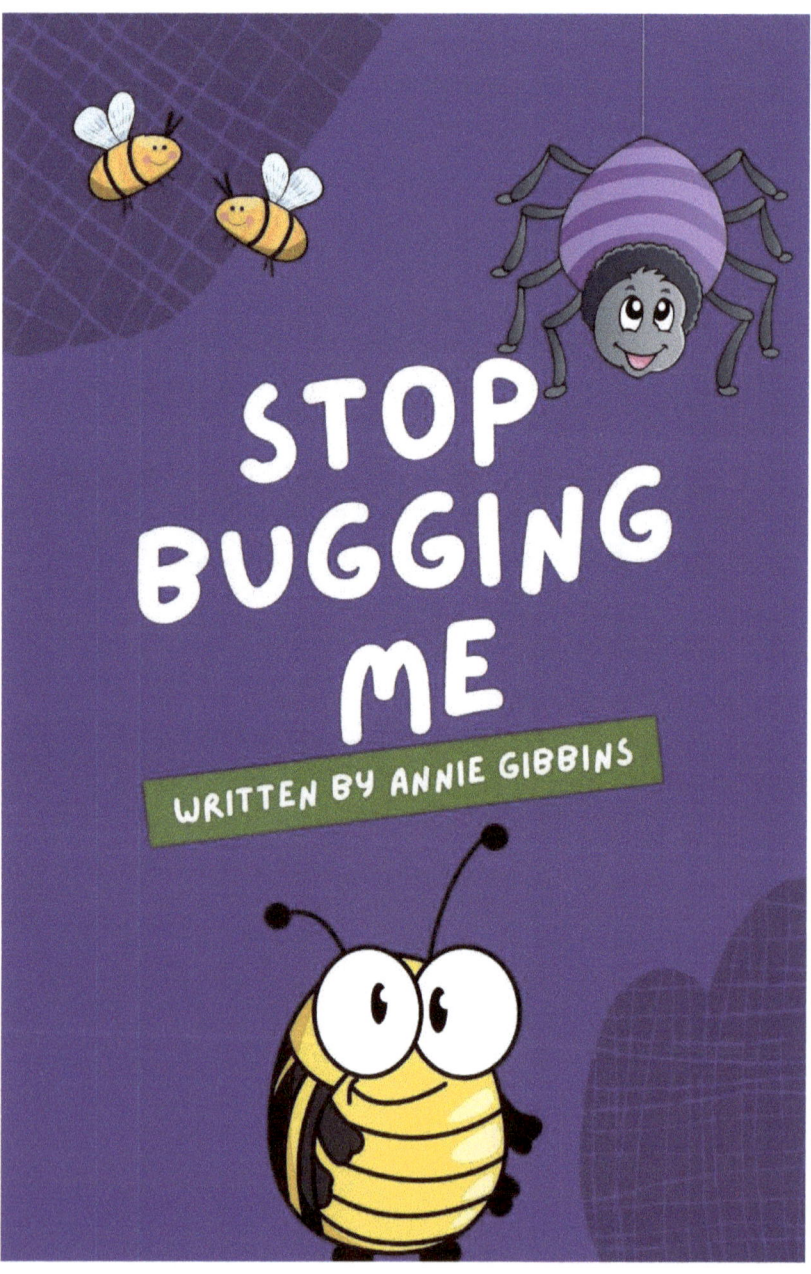

CHAPTER FIVE

WRITING STYLE AND VOICE

> *"Your writing voice is the unique way you express yourself on the page. It's your personality, your style, your tone. The more you write, the more it will emerge."* - Sharon Creech

Your writing style and voice can make or break a children's book. A captivating voice and unique style can keep young readers engaged and eager to read more. This chapter will provide tips for finding your writing voice, writing in a way that will engage children, as well as using humour and wordplay effectively.

Finding your Writing Voice

Finding your writing voice is an essential aspect of becoming a successful children's book author. Your writing voice is your unique writing style, which sets you apart from other authors. It is the way you express yourself through your writing, and it's crucial to develop a consistent voice that resonates with your young audience.

One tip for finding your writing voice is to write from the heart in a way that feels natural to you. Never be afraid to inject your personality into your writing and use your own experiences, observations and feelings to create a personal connection with your readers.

Another tip is to experiment with different writing styles and techniques. Read widely and study the works of successful children's book authors to gain inspiration and find what works for you. Try writing in different genres, using different points of view, and experimenting with different narrative structures.

When writing for children, it's essential to write in a way that engages and captivates their attention. Here are some tips to consider:
1. Use simple, straightforward language: Children have limited vocabulary and are still developing their reading skills. Use simple words and sentence structures that are easy to understand.
2. Write in an active voice: Active voice writing is more engaging and easier to follow than passive voice writing. Use action verbs to keep the story moving forward.
3. Create relatable characters: Children need to see themselves and their experiences represented in literature. Create characters that are diverse, multidimensional, and relatable.
4. Use sensory details: Sensory details, such as sight, sound, smell, taste and touch, can help children imagine and connect with the story's world.

Tips for Writing in a Way to Engage Children

When writing for children, it's essential to keep in mind that they have shorter attention spans and are less likely to engage with material that is overly complex or difficult to understand. Here are some tips for writing in a way that will engage children:

1. Use age-appropriate language: Use words and sentence structures that are appropriate for your target audience's age and reading level. Avoid using complex vocabulary or

convoluted sentence structures that may be difficult for children to understand.

2. Use active voice: Using active voice helps to make your writing more engaging and dynamic. It creates a sense of action and movement in your writing and makes it easier for young readers to follow along.
3. Keep sentences short: Short sentences are easier for children to understand and process. Long, complex sentences can be overwhelming and confusing for young readers.
4. Use descriptive language: Use vivid, descriptive language to create a strong sense of imagery in your writing. This can help to keep children engaged and make the story more memorable.
5. Use dialogue: Dialogue can help to bring characters to life and create a sense of personality and individuality. It also makes the story more interactive and engaging for young readers.
6. Incorporate humour: Children love to laugh, and incorporating humour into your writing can help to keep them engaged and interested. Just make sure that the humour is appropriate for your target audience and doesn't detract from the story.
7. Make it relatable: Children are more likely to engage with material that they can relate to. Try to incorporate situations, experiences and emotions that are familiar to your target audience.

Using Humour and Wordplay Effectively
Effectively using humour and wordplay can greatly enhance the quality of a children's book. Here are some tips for incorporating humour and wordplay into your writing:

1. Use age-appropriate humour: Be sure to keep the humour suitable for the age group you are writing for. Younger children may enjoy simple physical humour or silly jokes, while older

children may appreciate more nuanced and sophisticated humour.
2. Play with language: Use wordplay such as puns, alliteration, and rhyme, to make the text more engaging and memorable. This can also help with developing a unique voice and style.
3. Use humour to develop characters: Humorous situations and dialogue can reveal character traits and add depth to them. This can make characters more relatable and likeable to young readers.
4. Use humour to lighten heavy subjects: If you are dealing with serious or heavy subjects in your book, humour can be used as a tool to break up the tension and keep young readers engaged.
5. Avoid offensive or insensitive humour: It's important to be mindful of the potential impact of humour and avoid making offensive or insensitive jokes. This is especially important when writing for diverse audiences and addressing sensitive topics.

Key Takeaway

Finding your writing voice and developing a writing style that engages children is key to writing a successful children's book. Use a conversational tone, keep your language simple, and use humour and wordplay effectively to create an enjoyable and memorable reading experience for young readers.

Inspirational Cover Design

CHAPTER SIX

EDITING AND REVISING

> *"Editing is the most important part of writing. The first draft is just the beginning; it's in the editing process that your story truly comes to life."* - Stephen King

Writing a children's book is a creative and rewarding process, but it does not end with the completion of the first draft. Editing and revising are critical steps that help refine your ideas, polish your writing, ensuring your story is clear, engaging, and free from errors.

Self-Editing

Self-editing is an important first step in the editing and revising process. By reviewing your manuscript, yourself, you can identify areas that need improvement, before seeking feedback from others or working with an editor. Here are some tips for effective self-editing:

1. Take a break before editing: After finishing your first draft, step away from your manuscript for a few days, or even weeks. This break will give you distance from your work and allow you to approach it with fresh eyes.

2. Read your manuscript aloud: Reading your manuscript aloud can help you identify awkward phrasing, run-on sentences, and other grammatical errors you may not have noticed when reading silently.
3. Check for consistency: Check your manuscript for consistency in character traits, plot details and style. Make sure that your story flows logically and that the characters remain true to themselves throughout the story.
4. Eliminate unnecessary words: Be on the lookout for unnecessary words, phrases, or descriptions that can be eliminated without impacting the story. This will help tighten your prose and make your story more engaging.

Giving and Receiving Feedback

Getting feedback from others is an important step in the editing and revising process. Feedback can help you identify blind spots, improve your writing and refine your ideas.

Here are some tips for giving and receiving feedback:
1. Be specific and constructive: When giving feedback, be specific about what you liked and didn't like about the manuscript. Provide constructive criticism that is focused on improving the story rather than personal opinions.
2. Focus on the story: Keep the focus on the story, rather than the writer. Avoid criticising the writer personally or making assumptions about their intentions.
3. Keep an open mind: Be open to suggestions and willing to consider different perspectives. Feedback can be valuable even if you don't agree with it, as it can help you see your manuscript in a new light.
4. Avoid defensiveness: It's important not to get defensive when receiving feedback. Remember that the feedback is about the

5. manuscript and not about you personally. Try to view it as an opportunity to improve your writing.

Working with an Editor

If you plan to publish your children's book, working with an editor can be a valuable investment. An editor can help you refine your manuscript, identify areas that need improvement and provide guidance on the publishing process. Here are some tips for working with an editor:
1. Research potential editors: Look for editors who specialise in children's books and have experience working with authors in your genre.
2. Establish clear communication and expectations: Clearly communicate your expectations and goals to your editor. Make sure you both agree on the scope of the project, deadlines, and fees.
3. Be receptive to feedback and suggestions: Be open to feedback and suggestions from your editor. Remember that their goal is to help you improve your manuscript and create the best possible book.
4. Be open to making changes: Be willing to make changes to your manuscript based on your editor's feedback. Remember that the ultimate goal is to create the best possible book for your readers.

Key Takeaway

Editing and revising are critical steps in the writing process. Self-editing, GIVING? and receiving feedback, and working with an editor can all help you refine your ideas, improve your writing, and create a children's book that is engaging, polished, and ready for publication.

Inspirational Cover Design

CHAPTER SEVEN

ILLUSTRATIONS AND DESIGN

> *"Finding the right illustrator is like finding the perfect dance partner. Look for someone whose style complements your own, and who shares your creative vision."* - Grace Lin

Illustrations play a crucial role in children's books. They can capture a child's imagination, bring the story to life and add an extra layer of meaning to the text. In this chapter, we will discuss the importance of illustrations, finding an illustrator, creating your own illustrations, and tips for designing a visually appealing book.

The Role of Illustrations

Illustrations are more than just pretty pictures; they serve a vital purpose in children's books. They can help young readers visualise the story, understand complex concepts and build emotional connections with the characters. Illustrations can also help to break up long stretches of text, making the book more appealing and accessible to young readers.

Finding an Illustrator

If you're not an artist yourself, you'll need to find an illustrator to bring your story to life visually. There are a few ways to go about this:

1. Hire a professional illustrator: You can find professional illustrators through online marketplaces, or by asking for recommendations from other authors or publishers. Be sure to review their portfolios and find someone whose style matches the tone and style of your story.
2. Collaborate with an artist: If you have a friend or family member who is an artist, consider collaborating with them on your project. Be sure to discuss payment and compensation in advance, and establish clear communication and expectations.
3. Use stock illustrations: Some self-publishing platforms offer access to stock illustrations that you can use in your book. While this is a cost-effective option, be aware that these illustrations may not be exclusive to your book and may be used by other authors.

Creating Your Own Illustrations

If you have artistic talent and prefer to create your own illustrations, there are a few things to keep in mind:

1. Consistency: Aim for a consistent style and colour palette throughout the book to create a cohesive look.
2. Character design: Create distinct and memorable characters through drawings that will resonate with young readers.
3. Composition: Consider the layout and composition of your illustrations to ensure they are visually interesting and engaging.

Tips for Designing a Visually Appealing Book

Once you have your illustrations, it's important to consider how they will be presented in your book. Here are a few tips for designing a visually appealing book:

1. Choose an appropriate size: Consider the age of your target audience and choose a size that is comfortable for them to hold and read.
2. Use colour: Colourful illustrations can capture a child's attention and add to the visual appeal of the book.
3. Font and text: Choose a font that is easy to read and consider the placement and size of text, to ensure it does not detract from the illustrations.
4. Layout: Pay attention to the layout of your book, ensuring the illustrations are well-spaced and complement the text.
5. Cover design: Create an eye-catching cover that accurately represents the tone and content of your book. This is the first impression that potential readers will have, so it's important to make it shine.

Key Takeaway

Key illustrations and design play a vital role in children's books. Whether you hire a professional illustrator or create your own illustrations, it is important to pay attention to consistency, character design, composition and visual appeal. In doing so, you can create a book that not only engages young readers, but also leaves a lasting impression.

Inspirational Cover Design

CHAPTER EIGHT

PUBLISHING AND PROMOTION

> *"Building a brand is about more than just selling books. It's about creating a relationship with your readers and establishing yourself as a trusted voice in the industry."* - Marissa Meyer

After countless hours writing and perfecting your children's book manuscript, it's now time to think about publishing and promotion. This chapter will provide you with a comprehensive guide to the various publishing options available, effective marketing strategies to promote your book, as well as tips for building both a brand and a following.

Publishing Options

When it comes to publishing your children's book, you have several options to choose from. Each option has its pros and cons, and it's essential to weigh them up carefully to determine what is the best fit for you and your book. Here are the most common publishing options.

Traditional Publishing: In traditional publishing, you submit your manuscript to a publishing house, and if accepted, they handle the editing, design and distribution of your book. Although this option typically offers the most exposure and credibility, it can also be competitive and time-consuming.

Self-publishing: Self-publishing allows you to have complete control over the publishing process, from editing, to cover design, to distribution. While it offers more creative control, self-publishing requires a higher upfront investment and may not have the same level of exposure as traditional publishing.

Hybrid Publishing: Hybrid publishing combines the benefits of traditional and self-publishing. In this model, you pay a fee to work with a publishing company that offers editing, design and distribution services. While it may offer more creative control than traditional publishing, it can be more expensive than self-publishing.

Marketing Strategies

Once your book is published, you'll need to promote it to reach your target audience. A range of effective marketing strategies to consider are as follows.

Book Launch: A book launch is a great way to generate buzz for your book. It can be held in-person or online, and it's an opportunity to connect with potential readers and media.

Social Media: social media is a powerful tool for promoting your book. You can create an author page, share updates about your book, and connect with potential readers.

Book Reviews: Getting positive book reviews is critical for attracting new readers. Reach out to bloggers, book clubs and online review sites to request reviews.

Book Tours: A book tour involves visiting bookstores, schools and libraries to promote your book. Tours are also an opportunity to connect with potential readers and create buzz for your book.

Building a Brand and a Following

Building a brand and a following can help establish yourself as a credible author and increase the exposure of your book. In doing so, there are a range of tips to consider.

Author Website: Create a website to showcase your work, share your author bio and promote your book.

Email Newsletter: Start an email newsletter to keep your readers updated on your work and future promotional events.

Speaking Engagements: Speaking engagements are an opportunity to connect with potential readers, promote your book, as well as establish yourself as an authority in your field.

Social Media: Use social media to connect with potential readers, share updates about your book and build a following.

Key Takeaway

Publishing and promoting a children's book are a significant undertaking. It requires careful consideration of the various publishing options, effective marketing strategies, and the development of a brand and a following. By following the tips outlined in this chapter, you can increase your chances of success and create a book that engages and inspires young readers.

Inspirational Cover Design

CHAPTER NINE

CHALLENGES AND OBSTACLES YOU MAY ENCOUNTER

While writing a children's book is a dream that many people hold close to their hearts, the road to success is not always easy. Along the way, you may face numerous challenges that can make it difficult to achieve your goals. One of the most common of these, is the fear of rejection. As a writer, you pour your heart and soul into your work, only to face the possibility of rejection from publishers. But fear not, in this chapter, we will explore a number of challenges that writers face when writing a children's book and provide valuable tips on how to overcome them. So, let's dive in and learn how to tackle these obstacles head-on.

Finding Inspiration

One of the biggest challenges in writing a children's book is finding inspiration for a story that is engaging, relatable and appropriate for young readers. This can be especially difficult if you are new to writing or are struggling with writer's block.

Tip: To overcome this challenge, try brainstorming different ideas and topics that interest you, or draw from personal experiences or emotions. Consider what themes or messages you want to convey to young readers and think about how to weave them into a story. You can also read children's books for inspiration and see what elements make them successful.

Developing Characters

Creating memorable and relatable characters that resonate with young readers is essential for a successful children's book, but it can be challenging to develop unique and authentic characters.

Tip: Spend time getting to know your characters and their backstories, motivations, and personalities. Consider their age, gender, and cultural background and how these factors might influence their actions and beliefs. You can also interview children to get their perspectives on what makes a character interesting or relatable.

Plot and Structure

Developing a compelling plot and structure that holds the reader's attention can be challenging, especially if you are not familiar with the conventions of children's literature.

Tip: Study the structure of successful children's books and identify the key plot points and themes that make them successful. Consider the age range of your readers and ensure that your plot and structure are appropriate for their level of comprehension.

Writing Style and Voice

Finding your own unique writing style and voice that appeals to young readers can be challenging, especially if you are not familiar with the conventions of children's literature.

Tip: Read widely in the genre and identify the writing styles and voices that resonate with you. Experiment with different styles and voices until you find one that feels authentic and engaging. Consider your target audience and ensure that your writing style is appropriate for their age and level of comprehension.

Editing and Revising

Editing and revising your manuscript can be a daunting task, especially if you are not experienced in the publishing process.

Tip: Seek feedback from beta readers, critique partners, or professional editors, to identify areas that need improvement. Take a break from your manuscript and come back to it with fresh eyes to identify errors or inconsistencies. Be willing to make changes and revisions to improve the overall quality of your manuscript.

Illustrations and Design

Creating visually appealing illustrations that enhance your story can be a challenge, especially if you are not an artist or designer.

Tip: Work with a professional illustrator or designer who specialises in children's books. Collaborate with them to develop a visual style that complements your story and engages young readers. If you choose to create your own illustrations, practice regularly and seek feedback from others to improve your skills.

Publishing

Finding a publisher who is interested in your manuscript can be difficult, especially in a competitive market.

Tip: Research potential publishers who specialise in children's books and ensure that your manuscript aligns with their specific interests and guidelines. Consider self-publishing as an alternative and research the options available to you.

Promotion

Marketing and promoting your book can be a challenge, especially if you are not experienced in book promotion.

Tip: Develop a marketing plan that includes strategies for social media, book signings, and other promotional events. Collaborate with other authors or bloggers to increase your visibility and reach out to libraries or schools for potential speaking engagements.

Rejection: Rejection from Publishers

Rejection is one of the biggest challenges that writers face in the publishing industry, and this is especially true for those writing children's books. After spending countless hours developing your manuscript, it can be disheartening to receive a rejection letter from a publisher or literary agent.

Rejection can take many forms, from outright rejection letters to a lack of response from publishers or agents. It can be difficult to keep your spirits up and continue to pursue publication after receiving multiple rejections. However, it's important to remember that rejection is a normal part of the publishing process. Even famous authors such as J.K. Rowling and Stephen King faced countless rejection before finding success. The key to overcoming rejection is to stay persistent and keep adjusting and improving your manuscript.

Tip: One way to overcome the feelings associated with rejection is to seek feedback from other writers or writing groups. By getting constructive criticism, you can identify areas that need improvement and make changes to your manuscript. Another way is to consider self-publishing as an alternative option. With the rise of digital publishing platforms and print-on-demand services, self-publishing is a viable option that allows you to maintain creative control and potentially reach a wider audience.

Inspirational Cover Design

CHAPTER TEN

OVER TO YOU

I hope this beginner's guide helps you to write your own children's book. Remember to have fun, be creative, and most importantly of all, be persistent. As you have learnt, writing a children's book can be a challenging, yet fulfilling endeavour. It requires creativity, patience and a deep understanding of your audience. The different chapters in this book have outlined the essential elements of writing a successful children's book. From generating ideas to developing characters, plot and structure, writing style and voice, editing and revising, to illustrations and design, and finally publishing and promotion, each step is crucial in creating a book that will engage, inspire and educate young readers.

By following the tips and strategies provided in this book, you can bring your story to life and create a book that will captivate children's imaginations. Remember that writing a children's book is not just about writing an interesting story. It's about creating a world that children can escape into, characters they can relate to, and a story that they can connect with. The publishing industry is highly competitive, but with the right marketing and promotion, you can reach your target audience and build a loyal following.

Remember to stay true to your voice and your brand and be persistent in your efforts to promote your book. With dedication, hard work and a passion for writing, you can make your dream of publishing a children's book a reality.

And finally, consider Women's Biz Publishing as a resource for furthering your journey in writing and publishing children's books. We are committed to supporting and empowering authors, especially women, in achieving their goals and bringing their stories to life. Whether you need assistance with editing and revising, finding an illustrator, or navigating the publishing process, our team of experts is here to help. You can reach out to us at annie@womensbizglobal.com or visit womensbizpublishing.com for more information.

Inspirational Cover Design

BONUS MATERIAL

KEY ELEMENTS OF WRITING A CHILDREN'S BOOK

Title: The Little Writer's Adventure

Once upon a time, there was a little girl, named Emma, who loved to write stories. She had a big imagination and was always coming up with new ideas for her stories.

Chapter 1: Getting Started

Emma sat down at her desk with a pencil and paper, ready to start writing. She knew that she needed to come up with a great idea, so she closed her eyes and let her imagination run wild. Suddenly, she had an idea for a story about a magical unicorn who could fly.

Chapter 2: Developing the Plot

Emma started writing her story, but she quickly realised that she needed to develop the plot further. She thought about what her unicorn would do and what challenges it would face. She decided that her unicorn would be on a mission to save a lost princess from an evil sorcerer.

Chapter 3: Creating Memorable Characters

Emma knew that her story needed memorable characters, so she created a cast of characters to accompany her unicorn on its adventure. She created a brave knight, a wise old wizard, and a mischievous fairy. Each character had their own unique personality and added depth to her story.

Chapter 4: Using Dialogue to Advance the Story

As Emma continued writing her story, she realised that dialogue could be a powerful tool for advancing the plot. She used dialogue to show the relationships between her characters and to reveal their motivations. She also used dialogue to build tension and suspense.

Chapter 5: Revising and Editing

Once Emma had finished her story, she knew she needed to revise and edit the finished product. She took a break from her story for a 0few days and then came back to it with fresh eyes. She focused on the big picture elements, such as plot and character development, then edited for grammar and style.

Chapter 6: Publishing Your Story

Emma had a choice to make about how she wanted to publish her story. She could either send it to a traditional publisher, or self-publish it. She decided to self-publish and worked with professionals to help with editing, cover design and formatting. Finally, she launched her book and shared it with the world. Emma's book became a hit with young readers, and she became a successful children's book author. She learned that with hard work, persistence, and creativity, she could bring her stories to life and share them with the world.

So, What Did Emma Write About in Her Children's Book?

Emma wrote about a magical unicorn who goes on a mission to save a lost princess from an evil sorcerer. Along the way, the unicorn is accompanied by a brave knight, a wise old wizard, and a mischievous fairy. Together, they face many challenges and obstacles, but through their teamwork and determination, they are able to save the princess and defeat the sorcerer. The story is full of adventure, magic and friendship, and is sure to capture the imaginations of young readers.

Short Version: The Quest of the Magical Unicorn

Once upon a time, there was a magical unicorn, Sparkle, who lived in a magical kingdom far, far away. Sparkle had a special gift - she could fly. One day, she heard a cry for help coming from the forest. It was the voice of a lost princess, who had been kidnapped by an evil sorcerer. Without a second thought, Sparkle took off into the sky, determined to save the princess. As she flew over the forest, she spotted a brave knight, Sir Ryan, who was also on a quest to save the princess. Together, they decided to rescue her.

Together, Sparkle and Sir Ryan went on a dangerous mission to reach the sorcerer's castle. Along the way, they met a wise old wizard, Merlin, who joined them on their quest. They faced many challenges, including a treacherous river, a dark cave, and a maze of thorny bushes.

As they reached the castle, they faced the final obstacle - the sorcerer's powerful magic. Sparkle knew she had to use her gift of flight to outsmart the sorcerer. She soared high above the castle, distracting the sorcerer with her beautiful wings, while Sir Ryan and Merlin snuck into the castle to save the princess.

In the end, they were successful in their mission. They saved the princess and defeated the sorcerer. Sparkle, Sir Ryan, and Merlin returned to the kingdom as heroes and were celebrated by all the creatures in the land. And from that day on, Sparkle became known as the greatest hero of all, inspiring others to be brave, kind, and adventurous like her.

The End.

A More Detailed Version: The Quest of the Magical Unicorn

Once upon a time, in a faraway kingdom, there lived a magical unicorn named Sparkle. She was a beautiful creature, with a white coat that sparkled in the sunlight, and a mane and tail, made of shimmering rainbows. Sparkle had a special gift that set her apart from all the other creatures in the land - she could fly. And she loved nothing more than soaring high above the clouds, feeling the wind rush through her mane and the sun on her face.

One day, as Sparkle was flying over the kingdom, she heard a cry for help coming from the forest below. It was the voice of a lost princess, who had been kidnapped by an evil sorcerer. Sparkle knew she had to help the princess, and without a second thought, she took off into the sky, determined to save her.

As she flew over the forest, Sparkle spotted a brave knight, Sir Ryan who was also on a quest to save the princess. Sir Ryan was a tall, muscular man with a kind heart and a sharp mind. When Sparkle told him about the princess, Sir Ryan immediately agreed to join her on her mission.

Together, Sparkle and Sir Ryan flew over the forest, searching for any clues that would lead them to the princess. As they were flying, they heard rustling in the bushes below. They quickly landed and found a wise old wizard, Merlin, who had been searching for the princess as well. Merlin was an ancient man, with a long white beard and a twinkle in his eye. He told Sparkle and Sir Ryan that the princess had been taken to the sorcerer's castle, which was hidden deep in the forest.

Together, the three of them went on a dangerous adventure to reach the sorcerer's castle. Along the way, they faced many challenges and obstacles. They had to cross a treacherous river, navigate through a dark cave filled with bats, and make their way around a maze of thorny bushes. But through it all, Sparkle, Sir Ryan, and Merlin worked together as a team, using their unique skills and abilities to overcome each obstacle.

As they approached the sorcerer's castle, they realised that the final challenge would be the most difficult of all. The sorcerer had powerful magic, and it would take all of their skills and determination to defeat him. Sparkle knew that she had to use her gift of flight to outsmart the sorcerer. She soared high above the castle, distracting the sorcerer with her beautiful wings, while Sir Ryan and Merlin snuck into the castle to save the princess.

In the end, they were successful in their mission. They saved the princess and defeated the sorcerer. Sparkle, Sir Ryan and Merlin returned to the kingdom as heroes and were celebrated by all the creatures in the land. And from that day on, Sparkle became known as the greatest hero of all, inspiring others to be brave, kind, and adventurous like her.

The End.

Now let's See how Emma's Story could be written in 5 different styles.

Sample 1

The Quest of the Magical Unicorn

In a magical land far beyond our reach, there lived a unicorn unlike any other. Her name was Sparkle, and her coat shone brighter than the stars in the night sky. She possessed a rare talent that made her the envy of all who knew her - she could fly. She would take off into the sky whenever she pleased, feeling the wind beneath her wings and the sun on her back.

One day, Sparkle was soaring high above the kingdom, when she heard a cry for help coming from deep within the forest. It was the voice of a princess, who had been captured by an evil sorcerer. Sparkle knew she had to do something to save the princess, and without hesitation, she flew down to the forest floor to investigate.

There, she met a brave knight, Sir Ryan, who was also on a quest to save the princess. He was a tall and muscular man, with eyes that sparkled like diamonds. Sparkle knew he would be a valuable ally in their quest, and together they took to the skies.

As they flew, they stumbled upon a wise old wizard, Merlin, who was searching for the princess as well. Merlin was an ancient man with a long, white beard and a twinkle in his eye. He shared with them the location of the sorcerer's castle, and together the trio embarked on a dangerous adventure to rescue the princess.

Their journey was fraught with danger, from treacherous rivers to dark caves filled with bats. But Sparkle, Sir Ryan and Merlin faced each challenge with bravery and determination, using their unique abilities to overcome each obstacle.

As they approached the sorcerer's castle, Sparkle knew that their toughest challenge lay ahead. The sorcerer was powerful, and it would take all their combined strengths to defeat him. Sparkle used her gift of flight to distract the sorcerer, while Sir Ryan and Merlin snuck into the castle to rescue the princess.

In the end, they were successful in their mission. They saved the princess and defeated the sorcerer and returned to the kingdom as heroes. Sparkle, Sir Ryan, and Merlin's bravery and determination inspired all those who heard their story, and their legend lived on for generations to come.

The Quest of the Magical Unicorn was one that would never be forgotten, a story of bravery, adventure, and the enduring power of friendship.

The End.

Sample 2

Once upon a time, in a kingdom so grand,
There lived a unicorn, who could fly, you understand?
Her name was Sparkle, with a coat white as snow,
And a mane made of rainbows, oh, what a glow!

One day, as she soared through the sky,
She heard a cry for help and didn't know why.
A princess had been kidnapped, oh no!
By an evil sorcerer, who was full of woe.

Sparkle flew to the forest, where she met Sir Ryan,
A knight so brave, with muscles so lion.
They searched and searched, with no avail,
Until they met Merlin, the wise old male.

Together, the trio went on a quest,
To save the princess and give her rest.
They faced many challenges, like a river so wide,
And a dark cave filled with bats, which they had to abide.

But they kept going, with hearts full of fire,
Using their skills, they never did tire.
And then, they reached the sorcerer's castle so grand,
Their final challenge was now at hand.

The sorcerer had powerful magic, that was clear,
But Sparkle had a trick, which they had no fear.
She flew high, and distracted the foe,
While Sir Ryan and Merlin saved the princess, you know.

They defeated the sorcerer, and saved the day,
Returning to the kingdom, in a grand display.
Sparkle was a hero, known far and wide,

Inspiring all to be brave, and adventurous inside.
And so, the tale ends, with a lesson so true,
That when you work together, there's nothing you can't do.

The End.

Sample 3

I'm sorry, but I must begin by warning you that the following tale is not one of happiness and joy, but rather one of danger, peril, and adventure. If you are looking for a light-hearted story, then I suggest you stop reading now and look elsewhere. However, if you are prepared for what lies ahead, then I will proceed.

In a faraway kingdom, there once lived a magical unicorn by the name of Sparkle. This creature was not like any other, for she possessed a rare gift - the ability to fly. Her coat was as white as the clouds, and her mane and tail were made of shimmering rainbows that danced in the sunlight. But her most extraordinary attribute was her bravery. One day, as she soared high above the kingdom, she heard a cry for help coming from the forest below.

Without hesitation, Sparkle darted towards the source of the sound, and there she found a lost princess who had been kidnapped by an evil sorcerer. But Sparkle was not alone in her quest, for she met a brave knight, Sir Ryan, who joined her in her mission to rescue the princess. Together, they embarked on a treacherous journey that would take them through dark caves filled with bats, treacherous rivers, and mazes of thorny bushes. But they pressed on, determined to save the princess and defeat the evil sorcerer.

As they neared the sorcerer's castle, they faced their most daunting challenge yet. The sorcerer was a master of dark magic and defeating him would not be an easy task. But Sparkle was determined to use her gift of flight to outsmart him. She soared high above the castle, her wings fluttering in the wind, while Sir Ryan and a wise old wizard, Merlin, they had met along the way, snuck into the castle to save the princess.

Finally, after a long and perilous journey, they emerged victorious. The princess was rescued, and the sorcerer was defeated. Sparkle, Sir Ryan and Merlin returned to the kingdom as heroes, celebrated by all the creatures in the land.

And so, dear reader, let this story serve as a reminder that even in the face of danger and darkness, there is always hope. For as long as there are brave and kind-hearted creatures like Sparkle, there will always be a chance to triumph over evil and restore light to a darkened world.

The End.

Sample 4

Once upon a time, there was a unicorn named Sparkle who could fly! Sparkle had a pretty mane and tail, with all the colours of a rainbow, and her body was white, just like a cloud. Everyone loved to see her fly over town. One day, Sparkle heard a princess shouting for help. The princess had been taken by an evil sorcerer and put in a castle. Sparkle knew she had to help, so she decided to go on a rescue mission.

Along the way, she met a brave knight, Sir Ryan and a wise wizard, Merlin, who also wanted to help the princess. Together, they travelled through a forest, a river, and a maze to reach the castle. The sorcerer was strong, but Sparkle had a plan. She flew around the castle to distract him, while Sir Ryan and Merlin ran inside and saved the princess.

They beat the sorcerer and rescued the princess, and everyone in the kingdom was happy. Sparkle became the greatest unicorn of all and made others want to be brave and have adventures, just like her.

The End

Sample 5

So, once upon a time, there was this totally cool unicorn named Sparkle. She had a horn that could light up like a disco ball and wings that flapped faster than a hummingbird. She lived in this amazing forest, where all the animals loved to dance and make silly faces.

One day, while Sparkle was flying around the forest, she heard this really loud cry for help. It was coming from this big castle nearby, where a princess had been taken by an evil sorcerer. Sparkle knew she had to do something to save the princess and make things right.

With her heart racing and her wings flapping like crazy, Sparkle flew towards the castle. She knew it wouldn't be easy, but she was determined to use all her super cool powers to save the day. As she got closer to the castle, she saw some guards standing at the entrance. But Sparkle was not scared. She used her neon horn to make a super cool light show that distracted the guards and let her sneak in unnoticed.

Inside the castle, Sparkle used her awesome powers to navigate through the dark and twisty corridors. She could hear the princess crying out for help, and she knew she had to find her fast. Finally, Sparkle found the princess locked in this tower room, guarded by a really big dragon. Sparkle knew she had to be brave and face the dragon head on. With a big smile on her face, Sparkle charged towards the dragon. She used her neon horn to blast the dragon with awesome music, then swooped down to grab the princess and carry her to safety.

As Sparkle flew back to her forest home with the princess, all the animals cheered and danced to her super cool tunes. From that day forward, Sparkle was known as the coolest unicorn in all the land. The princess could not stop giggling at Sparkle's silly antics, and they became the best of friends. They went on all sorts of fun adventures together and had the best time ever. And that's how Sparkle the totally cool unicorn saved the princess and became a hero. Yay!

The End.

Now that you have the tools and knowledge to write a children's book, it's time to find your own unique voice and style. So, what's your writing style?

Only you can answer that question, but with dedication, practice, and perseverance, you will be able to develop your own unique voice and style that will captivate and engage young readers.

Think about what inspires you, what topics you are passionate about and the kind of stories you want to tell. Consider the different writing techniques and styles you have learned and how you can incorporate them into your own work.

Remember, the most important thing is to write from the heart and to stay true to yourself. Do not be afraid to take risks and try new things, as that's how you'll grow and improve as a writer.

Thank you for reading!

ABOUT THE AUTHOR

Annie Gibbins is a true Renaissance woman, with accomplishments in every facet of the business world. As an acclaimed TV and podcast host, keynote speaker, #1 best-selling author, publisher, and business mentor, Annie has established herself as a leading voice for women in business. Despite her numerous accomplishments, Annie's story is one of resilience and determination. She has successfully raised a family of five, including two sets of twins born only 26 months apart, all while building an incredible 7-figure business empire. Through Women's Biz Global, Annie has mentored countless women from around the world, helping them to achieve their goals and reach their full potential by calling out limiting beliefs, clarifying purpose, and developing strong business practices. Annie's story is a shining example of the incredible heights that can be achieved with hard work, dedication, and the right mindset. Her journey inspires women everywhere to break down barriers and achieve their wildest dreams. To connect with Annie to assist you with building up your business brand reach out to www.womensbizglobal.com.

www.ingramcontent.com/pod-product-compliance
Lightning Source LLC
Chambersburg PA
CBHW041314110526
44591CB00022B/2911